Ripley Readers

All true and unbelievable!

Learning to read. Reading to learn!

LEVEL ONE Sounding It Out Preschool–Kindergarten
For kids who know their alphabet and are starting to sound out words.

learning sight words • beginning reading • sounding out words

LEVEL TWO Reading with Help Preschool–Grade 1
For kids who know sight words and are learning to sound out new words.

expanding vocabulary • building confidence • sounding out bigger words

LEVEL THREE Independent Reading Grades 1–3
For kids who are beginning to read on their own.

introducing paragraphs • challenging vocabulary • reading for comprehension

LEVEL FOUR Chapters Grades 2–4
For confident readers who enjoy a mixture of images and story.

reading for learning • more complex content • feeding curiosity

Ripley Readers Designed to help kids build their reading skills and confidence at any level, this program offers a variety of fun, entertaining, and unbelievable topics to interest even the most reluctant readers. With stories and information that will spark their curiosity, each book will motivate them to start and keep reading.

Vice President, Licensing & Publishing Amanda Joiner
Editorial Manager Carrie Bolin

Editor Jessica Firpi
Writer Korynn Wible-Freels
Designer Rose Audette
Reprographics Bob Prohaska

Published by Ripley Publishing 2020

10 9 8 7 6 5 4 3 2 1

Copyright © 2020 Ripley Publishing

ISBN: 978-1-60991-448-6

For more information regarding permission, contact:
VP Licensing & Publishing
Ripley Entertainment Inc.
7576 Kingspointe Parkway, Suite 188
Orlando, Florida 32819

Email: publishing@ripleys.com
www.ripleys.com/books
Manufactured in China in January 2020.

First Printing

Library of Congress Control Number:
2019942271

PUBLISHER'S NOTE
While every effort has been made to verify the accuracy of the entries in this book, the Publisher cannot be held responsible for any errors contained in the work. They would be glad to receive any information from readers.

Ripley Readers

Pets

All true and unbelievable!

RIPLEY
PUBLISHING

a Jim Pattison Company

From puppies to guppies, there are all kinds of pets.

Let's learn about some of our friends with fur, feathers, and fins!

There are almost 90 million pet dogs in the United States!

The most popular breed is a Labrador. Labs come in three colors: black, brown, and yellow.

Believe it or not... A basenji does not bark. It yodels!

A Chihuahua
only weighs
six pounds!

A greyhound can run up to
43 miles per hour!

Did you know that cats can sleep for 15 hours a day?

Here is another fun fact: people in ancient Egypt used to worship cats!

Cats rock!

These kitties are in a band called The Rock Cats.

Some people like having fish as pets because they think that fish are good luck charms.

A baby fish is called a fry, and a group of fish is called a school. In the wild, a goldfish can live for 25 years!

Did you know that some fish glow in the dark?

They come in a bunch of colors:
red, green, orange, blue, purple,

Birds make great pets.
Some can mimic what you say.

African grey parrots can say more than 1,000 different words, and they are almost as smart as you are!

People like chickens as pets, too.

The silkie chicken looks like it is wearing a fur coat! Penny the silkie chicken is best friends with Roo the dog.

Hamsters, guinea pigs, rats, and mice are all rodents. Rodents make good class pets.

Their babies are called pups. A little dwarf hamster only grows two inches long!

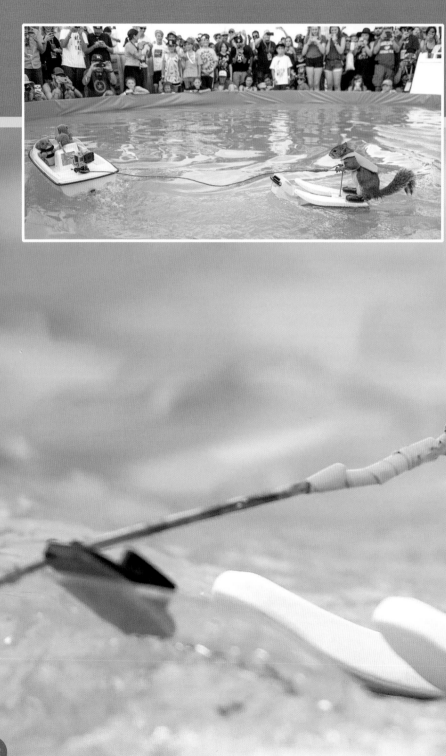

Can you train your pet to water ski like Twiggy the squirrel?

How do you tell a turtle and a tortoise apart? A turtle likes water, but a tortoise likes land!

Turtles, tortoises, snakes, and lizards are all reptiles. A pet python can grow up to 20 feet long!

Believe it or not... You can tell if a chameleon is happy, mad, or scared by its color!

A gecko can hang from one toe!

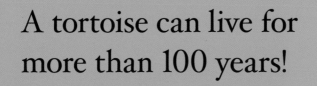

A tortoise can live for more than 100 years!

A rabbit can also be called a bunny or a hare. There are 60 kinds of pet rabbits!

Have you heard of a lop? It is a rabbit with floppy ears.

Look at this gentle giant! Darius is the world's biggest bunny. He is 46 pounds and eats more than 4,000 carrots a year!

Ready for More?

Ripley Readers feature unbelievable but true facts and stories!

LEVEL ONE Sounding it out

LEVEL TWO Reading with help

LEVEL THREE Independent reading

LEVEL FOUR Chapters

Sharks!

Trucks!

Pets

Shipwrecks

Weather

Horses

Bizarre Buildings

Dinosaurs!

For more information about Ripley's Believe It or Not!, go to www.ripleys.com